The Little Book of Treasure Baskets

Collections of objects for babies and children

Written by Ann Roberts
with
Sally Featherstone

Illustrations by Isabel Barnbrook

The Little Book of Treasure Baskets

ISBN 1 904187 05 6

First published in Great Britain by Featherstone Education Ltd, January 2002
Reprinted April 2002
Reprinted with minor revisions July 2002

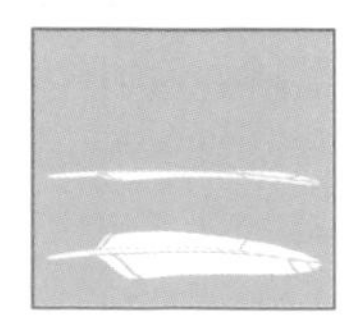

Contents

Treasure Baskets

In writing this book, we recognise the work of Elinor Goldschmied, whose writing and advice on treasure baskets has inspired many parents, carers and teachers, and encouraged them to give children natural objects to play with and explore.

The central theme of this Little Book is the way in which practitioners and parents can use baskets of objects to:

* encourage children to use of all their senses
* introduce the children to a wide range of natural materials
* balance the use of bright colours and man made materials with the subtle colours, textures and shapes of natural objects
* use collections of familiar objects to stimulate play
* provide opportunities for children to make choices and develop preferences from a very young age
* stimulate movement, communication and language through simple materials.

The book is in three sections:

Section 1 explores the use of Treasure Baskets with babies from the time when they can first sit up propped by cushions until the time they begin to crawl, stand and walk. During this time, the baskets can be adapted to meet the growing interests and needs of the baby. In this section we also offer suggestions about the contents of the baskets, how children should be positioned and supported when using them, and the role of the adult who is with them.

Section 2 covers the use of a treasure basket approach with older children - including those in the Foundation Stage. At this stage, Treasure Baskets can contribute to all the areas of learning.

Section 3 contains advice on selection, storage and maintenance of collections.

What are Treasure Baskets, and how can we use them with babies?

Treasure Baskets for babies can help them to:

* explore natural objects, textures and colours, using all their senses
* develop attention and concentration
* practice and refine their fine motor control and eye/hand co-ordination
* make simple choices and develop preferences
* explore and develop current schemas or ways of learning

Babies can explore treasure baskets from the time when they can first sit, propped by cushions for steadiness. At this stage, babies are 'rooted to the spot' and often get frustrated by their inability to reach the things they can see. They are learning fast, and need to be stimulated.

Elinor Goldschmied says "When planning a baby's diet, we give great attention to her menu, offering the range and quality essential for her daily nutrition and rapid growth. But what about her mental diet, which nurtures her developing capacity to use eyes, hands and mouth in concentrated activity?"

Treasure Baskets for babies contain collections of objects that are usually natural or made from natural materials. The world of bright colours and man made materials bombards children from birth, but there is now evidence that young children often respond more intensely to natural materials and more muted colours. These enable babies to explore on the texture, taste, smell and sound of objects, not just the look of them.

Once you have seen a baby engrossed in a treasure basket, you will realise the power the activity has. Babies are often absorbed in playing for as much as an hour with a basket, selecting, rejecting and exploring the objects with their whole bodies.

None of the objects in these first collections is a purpose made toy. Most are easily collected from around the house or setting, or can be bought cheaply from hardware or household shop.

The Treasure Basket itself is usually made from willow, wicker, straw, raffia or other natural woven material. It has a broad base and a big opening at the top, so the baby can see the contents and reach easily into the basket. The basket must be stable enough for the child to rest his or her arm on the edge without tipping it over or toppling over themselves! Elinor Goldschmied recommends a basket not less than 14" (351mm) in diameter and 4-5" (101-125mm) deep.

Treasure Baskets can have handles (as long as they don't get in the child's way), and are usually round or oval in shape. However, baskets for older children can be any shape, with or without lids, fasteners or dividers. When using Treasure Baskets in a nursery or pre-school, some practitioners have eased storage problems by having a small number of baskets, and storing the collections of contents in a series of drawstring bags, hung on hooks in a cupboard or on the wall.

The basic sensory collections in Part 1 can be extended and rearranged by you to further stimulate and interest the children.

Using the Basket

* Fill the basket with objects - the fuller the better.

* Seat the baby or babies sideways at the basket, so they can rest an elbow on the edge of the basket

* Sit nearby, so you can watch. Only intervene if they clearly need your attention.

What is the role of the adult in Treasure Basket experiences?

There is no doubt that Treasure Baskets will make an impact on a child - if they are introduced, offered and developed sensitively.

Adults should be attentive during Treasure Basket sessions, but should not intervene, except to ensure safety and maintain social contact with the baby. It is recommended that adults do not participate in the Treasure Basket sessions , even to start the play off. The object of the activity is for the baby to explore the contents of the basket in her/his own time, without adult interference. If s/he decides to spend half an hour exploring the qualities of a wooden spoon, this is his/her decision.

At this age, babies need to maintain some eye contact and what Elinor Goldschmied describes as 'friendly company and emotional anchorage'. This means that far from being ignored, babies have the chance to be independent in their play, often engaging for long periods with the items in their basket, and secure in the knowledge that an adult is nearby.

Adults are sometimes anxious that babies will hurt themselves or others with the items in the basket, some of which are hard or heavy. It is worth remembering that a baby who can just sit, while they can grasp or lift a heavy object such as a smooth stone, they are unlikely to be able to hurt themselves or others with it!

As babies become more agile and dexterous, you should review the contents of the basket and the growing competences of the child to ensure that the children cannot damage themselves or others as they explore.

Schemas and the Treasure Basket philosophy

What is a schema?

Schemas are usually described as generalised patterns of behaviour, the repeated behaviours we observe as we watch children play and investigate their surroundings.

Research suggests that these actions are pieces of a jigsaw which children are building up in their brain - repeating patterns of behaviour in a systematic way, exploring actions and thinking about those actions.

Schemas cut across gender, culture and race, and they do not follow predictable patterns or appear in any particular order. Some children show no evidence of schemas in their behaviour, some have several different schema at one time, sometimes schematic behaviour happens only at home or only in the setting. They occur in all aspects of children's play, and can teach us how some children learn.

Some **frequently observed schema** include:

* transporting (carrying items from one place to another, perhaps using a truck, pram, bag, purse or box)
* positioning (placing objects carefully)
* orientation (turning and placing objects)
* horizontality, verticality, diagonality, circularity (in building, drawing or mark making)
* enclosure (making enclosures with bricks, blocks, crates etc)
* enveloping or wrapping (putting things in bags, wrapping things)
* rotation (turning keys, knobs, wheels, taps)
* connection (joining things together)
* ordering
* transforming

Practitioners could support children's learning with relevant collections of objects to support schemas they observe in their group.

Principles for using Treasure Baskets as a resource linked to schema.

* Resources which support children's schematic needs should be both available and accessible.
* The collections should be varied and should contain duplicate items.
* Treasure Basket work should support both stability and change.
* Children need freedom to plan, discuss and develop their own learning strategies - practitioners should be flexible and accepting of changes and possible additions from children!

Supporting and extending schema through Treasure Baskets.

Treasure Baskets are a useful way to promote schema when:

* Positive adult attitudes support the constant repetition which can be a feature of any schema.
* An attractive environment with accessible objects encourages children of all ages to select their own resources, or at least to see and gesture their needs.
* Drapes, carpet squares, wood or mirror tiles enhance presentation, making basket work a valued part of your setting.
* Consistent and regular staff observation supports progression and language development as well as locating the emergence of new schemas.
* Quality time is allocated to basket work. This is a crucial element of the approach, and will enhance the benefits for children.

Involving parents in Treasure Basket work is vital - they need to understand the importance of the work and many will want to get involved in observing their children, collecting a home based Treasure Basket for their child, or perhaps borrowing baskets of items from your Toy Library.

Treasure Baskets, Schema & Special Educational Needs

Children with special needs and disabilities find Treasure Baskets a wonderful resource to explore - there are no right answers and no prescribed outcomes!

Children with special needs can really benefit from Treasure Baskets. Whether the child has moderate or severe physical or learning difficulties, the use of small specific collections of objects can help to target manipulative or sensory needs. Perfumes, textures, sound and movement can also be incorporated in the collections, depending on the needs of the individual child.

Children with special needs, particularly those children who have profound or communication difficulties, often demonstrate strong schema, and identifying these can provide a real breakthrough in meeting their needs. Treasure Baskets, with their emphasis on natural, context free materials give them an immediate appeal and lasting popularity.

More structured toys and materials often prove unacceptable to SEN children, who may find the constraints of such toys frustrating. Treasure Baskets provide flexible and varied stimuli, which can be varied according to the current schema, needs or interests of an individual child, while costing little and being easily stored. Treasure Baskets encourage interaction, maintain self esteem and improve motivation. Baskets and other containers can be used on wheelchair and buggy trays, with standing frames, on blankets and beanbags.

Children with special needs may require gentle adult assistance in exploring the contents of the basket, but adults should try to avoid dominating a child's experience by influencing what the child selects, or talking too much about the objects.

How do I ensure the safety of the objects in the baskets?

Of course babies and young children should always have hygienic and safe playthings. As with all other equipment, Treasure Baskets should be regularly checked and cleaned. the contents should also be checked for damage, splinters and sharp edges or points.

Some hints:

* remember, at this age babies will be able to grasp and hold the objects, but are unlikely to be able to hit or poke with them
* if you are not sure about the safety or hygiene of a particular object - don't include it
* if you are worried about the baby swallowing an object - try to swallow it yourself - if you can't they won't be able to!
* make sure the items are '**washable, wipeable or disposable**' (Elinor Goldschmied's words), and throw away disposable items after each use
* be vigilant and intervene if you are worried about a particular item when it is in use.

NB *When using the treasure basket approach with older children, or with babies when older children are present,you will need to look carefully at the match of objects to the maturity and development of the children.*

The Touch Basket

Touch plays a very important part in the life of young babies. Because it is well developed even at birth, it provides babies with more immediate access to their world than any other sense, and this is why it is the first in the senses collection.

Touch is essential to a baby's development. It obviously has an effect on sensory motor development, but it also has a potent influence over their physical growth, their emotional development and cognitive potential. Touch is also connected with the immune system, affecting health and physical wellbeing.

The touch basket promotes exploration of texture, shape, weight, and of coldness, smoothness and pattern. These are all concepts relevant to babies and nursery aged children.

Try some of these **natural objects**:

* fir cones of various sizes and types
* shells of a range of types and sizes
* gourds (either fresh or dried) in different sizes and textures of skin
* big feathers
* pumice stone
* loofah
* natural sponge
* pebbles
* driftwood
* corks
* a short length of rope

Disposables:

* a lemon
* an orange
* an apple
* a pomegranate
* cardboard tubes
* paper (tissue, greaseproof, foil, kitchen roll etc)

Try adding some of these **objects**:

* a baby or child's shoe
* a nail brush
* a shaving brush
* a small bottle brush
* a hairbrush
* a velvet powder puff
* a small teddy bear
* a leather purse (if culturally acceptable)
* a triangle
* a fur ball
* a tea strainer
* an avocado pear stone
* a short piece of chain
* a small wooden bowl
* a walnut
* a raffia coaster

The 'Touch Wood' Basket

This basket is filled with things made of wood. Wood provides children with enjoyable sensory experiences. The feel, the smell (and even the taste) of wood is a pleasure to most, and will encourage exploration by all the senses. Touching or stroking wood has a calming effect on some children, as they explore its curves and surfaces.

Try to provide a variety of different woods, with a range of grains, patterns and colours. Look in your kitchen drawer or utensil holder, or take a walk to collect natural wooden items. Driftwood from the seaside is always a good addition.

Once your collection has begun, you will notice the natural, neutral appearance of the basket, giving a calming contrast to the bright colours of most toys.

Some items to collect:

* pine cones
* driftwood
* small offcuts from a DIY shop or carpenter
* flooring samples
* pieces of bark
* large curly shavings
* short lengths of broomstick
* wooden spoons and spatulas
* large nuts
* small sticks
* wooden eggs
* plain wood pencils
* wooden nesting dolls
* wooden blocks
* cotton reels (wooden)

* castanets
* a small boat
* wooden fruit
* a baby rattle
* chopsticks
* salad servers
* wooden bracelets

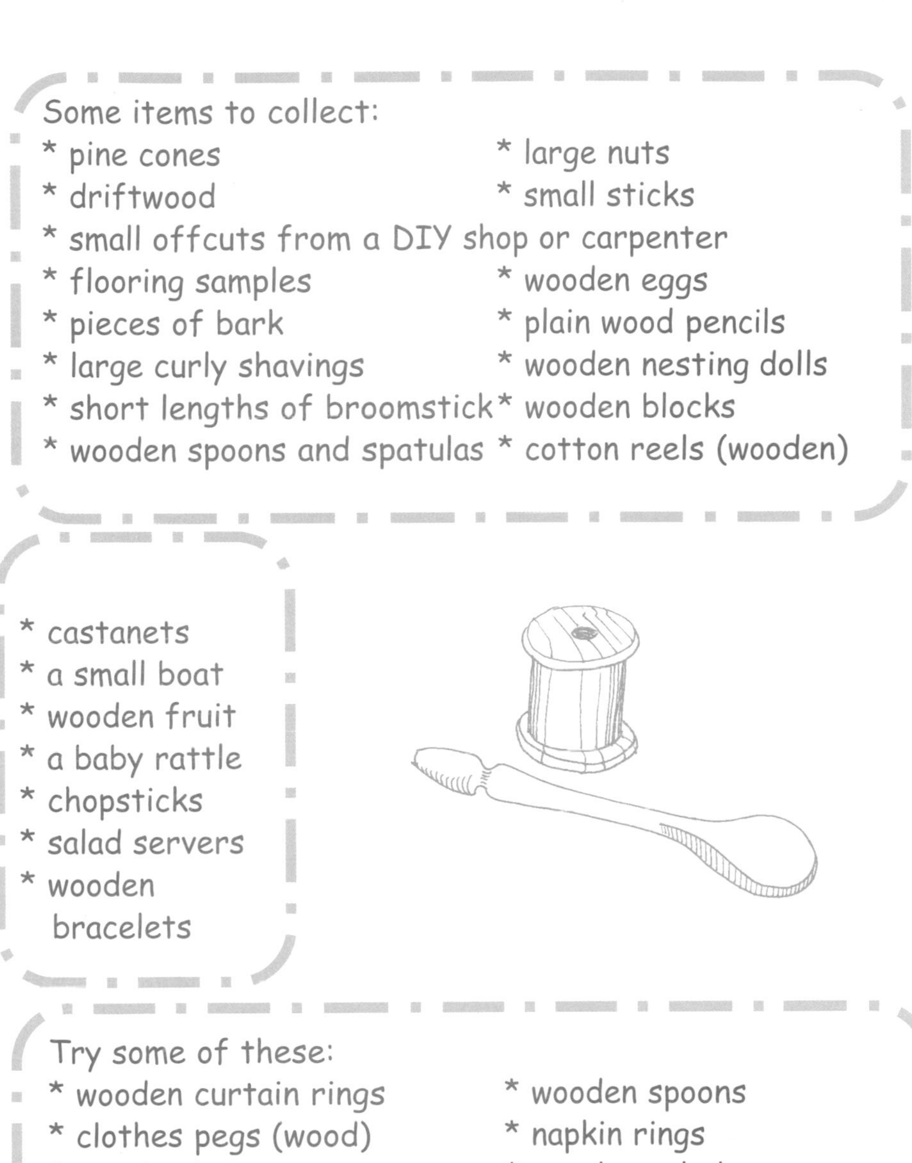

Try some of these:

* wooden curtain rings
* clothes pegs (wood)
* wooden boxes
* small bowls
* egg cup
* small wooden toys
* pastry crimper
* salt and pepper pots
* wooden spoons
* napkin rings
* wooden salad servers
* wooden beads
* corks (various)
* honey dipper
* small rolling pin
* coasters

Rolling Along

From the age of eight or nine months children are showing signs of moving about and crawling - exploring the world further. As children begin to move about, they become interested in other things that move too.

Stimulating items that roll and need chasing engage children and encourage movement in them. A collection of things that roll will support other collections and may be made up from them.

This collection can also be successfully used with older children to explore movement, test and talk about the properties of objects, how they roll and which roll best, sorting rollers and 'non rollers'.

As with all collections, these objects must be regularly wiped or washed to keep them free of dust, dirt and germs.

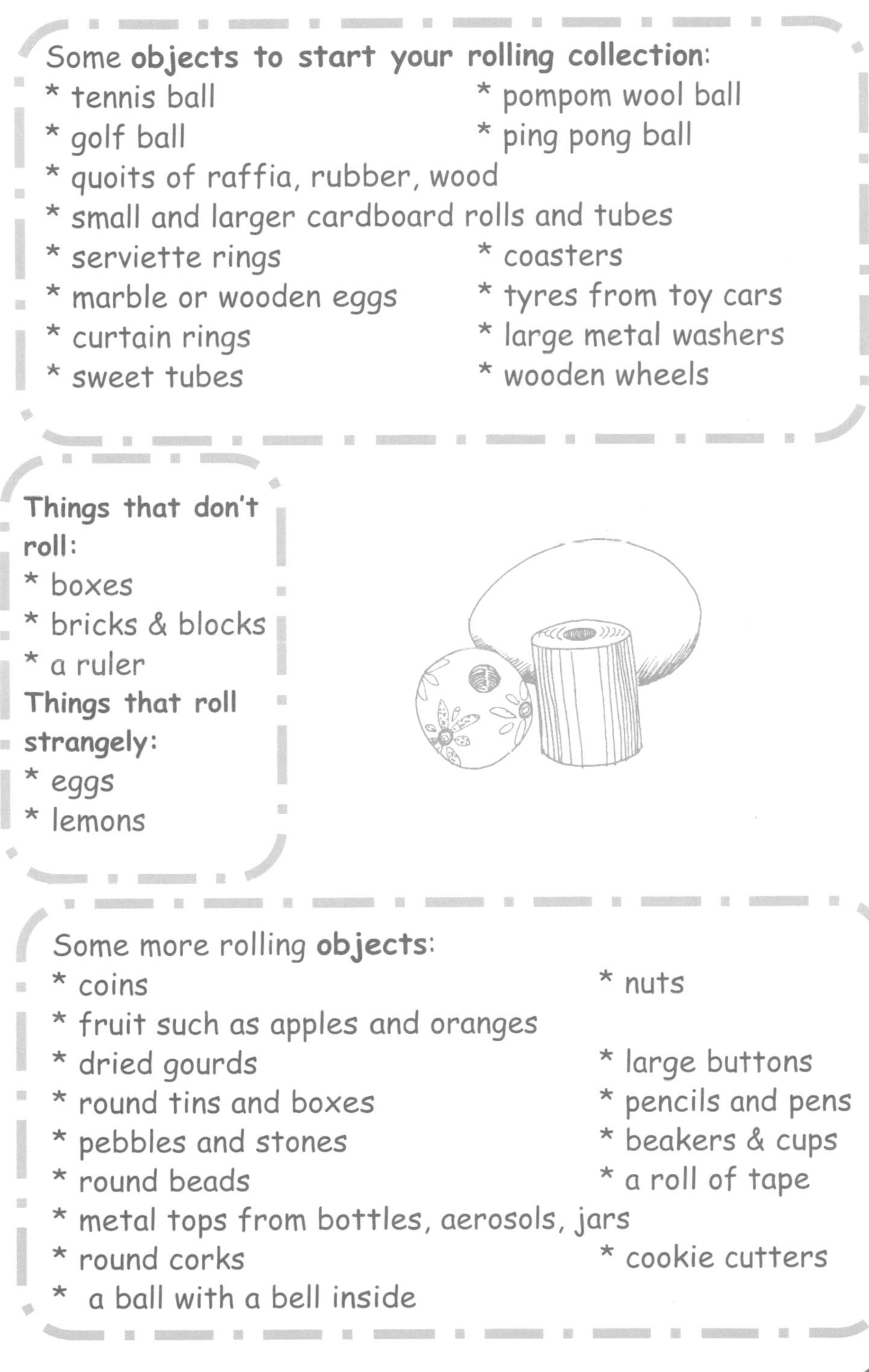

Some **objects to start your rolling collection**:

* tennis ball
* pompom wool ball
* golf ball
* ping pong ball
* quoits of raffia, rubber, wood
* small and larger cardboard rolls and tubes
* serviette rings
* coasters
* marble or wooden eggs
* tyres from toy cars
* curtain rings
* large metal washers
* sweet tubes
* wooden wheels

Things that don't roll:

* boxes
* bricks & blocks
* a ruler

Things that roll strangely:

* eggs
* lemons

Some more rolling **objects**:

* coins
* nuts
* fruit such as apples and oranges
* dried gourds
* large buttons
* round tins and boxes
* pencils and pens
* pebbles and stones
* beakers & cups
* round beads
* a roll of tape
* metal tops from bottles, aerosols, jars
* round corks
* cookie cutters
* a ball with a bell inside

The Sound of Metal

Metal objects are essential for most treasure baskets; this collection is a basket full of metal objects, many of which can be found in the kitchen.

Metal objects are fascinating to babies and young children. The shaking of a bunch of keys can attract the attention of a baby, even if she is crying. Spoons, keys, silver utensils all have handles to be grasped and reflections to be explored. The coldness of metal is another feature as the sense of touch is stimulated. The many sounds of metal vary from a jingle to a crash.

Watch the child careful select an item such as a plug on a chain and carefully replace it with amazing concentration and accuracy. Be aware! This basket makes a noise!

Try some of these **familiar objects**:

* spoons of various sizes and shapes
* keys in bunches on strings and rings
* keyrings strung together
* a plug with a chain attached
* small whisks
* a tea strainer
* metal cruet set
* bulldog clips
* costume jewellery
* mirror with metal frame
* tin lids
* a metal ash tray
* small baking tins
* a garlic press

Some musical instruments:

* a triangle
* bells
* a small cymbal
* a chime bar
* wind chimes
* a bike bell
* a harmonica

Try some of these **more unusual objects**:

* a dog chain
* a whistle on a chain
* a lemon press
* a bunch of bells
* curtain rings
* a small metal funnel
* a potato masher
* a metal jug
* a small saucepan with lid
* tins with lids
* a small sieve
* a metal toy car
* child's garden trowel
* a short piece of chain
* a large metal bolt (new)
* a doorknob

NB - you could spray a basket silver for this collection

The Bathroom Basket

Modern bathrooms are good sources of natural materials - you will find wood, steel, rubber, bristle, cotton, wool, shell, as well as natural perfumes and oils. This basket could be used to explore scents as well as taste, touch, sight and hearing.

For younger children, the basket will be a sensory exploration. Older children will begin to see the connection between the items in the basket and the care of our bodies, leading to discussions of health and hygiene.

Containers within the collection will allow for emptying and filling, pouring and tipping, thus expanding wrist and arm movements.

Try some of these **natural objects**:

* plugs and chains
* pieces of pumice stone
* a small metal soap holder
* pieces of loofah
* nail brush
* tooth brush
* pieces of cork
* metal dishes
* a metal beaker
* bath brush
* large bottle tops
* small baskets
* big stones and pebbles

Fabrics:

* a piece of towelling
* a flannel
* a piece of woollen cloth or fleece
* cotton wool

Try some of these **objects and scents**:

* empty perfume bottles (thick glass jars only)
* a makeup brush
* a shaving brush
* a stress roller
* shells
* a large powder puff
* nail file
* cloth bag of pot pourri
* dried flowers
* a small wooden boat
* cups and mugs
* funnels
* emery board
* small cloth bags with lavender, cloves, rosemary etc.

The Brush Basket

Brushes come in all shapes and sizes, with soft and stiffer bristles. With a bit of thought and imagination, you will be surprised how many brushes you can collect for this basket!

Some will be soft and tickly, and babies will love to stroke the sensitive skin of their cheeks, hands or feet with them. Brushing and stroking has a calming effect, so the basket could be offered when a child has become over stimulated or excited.

The types, sizes and shapes of the different brushes will give practice in holding and manipulating objects. Older children will often mime the action as they handle each brush.

NB Some brushes have long handles or sharp ends and it may be safer to cut these down before adding them to the basket.

Try some of these **brushes**:

* shaving brush
* hairbrush (with natural bristles and wooden back)
* baby's hairbrush
* pastry brush with wooden handle
* dustpan brush (wooden handle)
* small shoe brushes (several)
* makeup brushes
* painting brushes

Why not add some laminated pictures

* a baby
* a mother
* a father
* a boy
* a girl
* a dog
* a cat

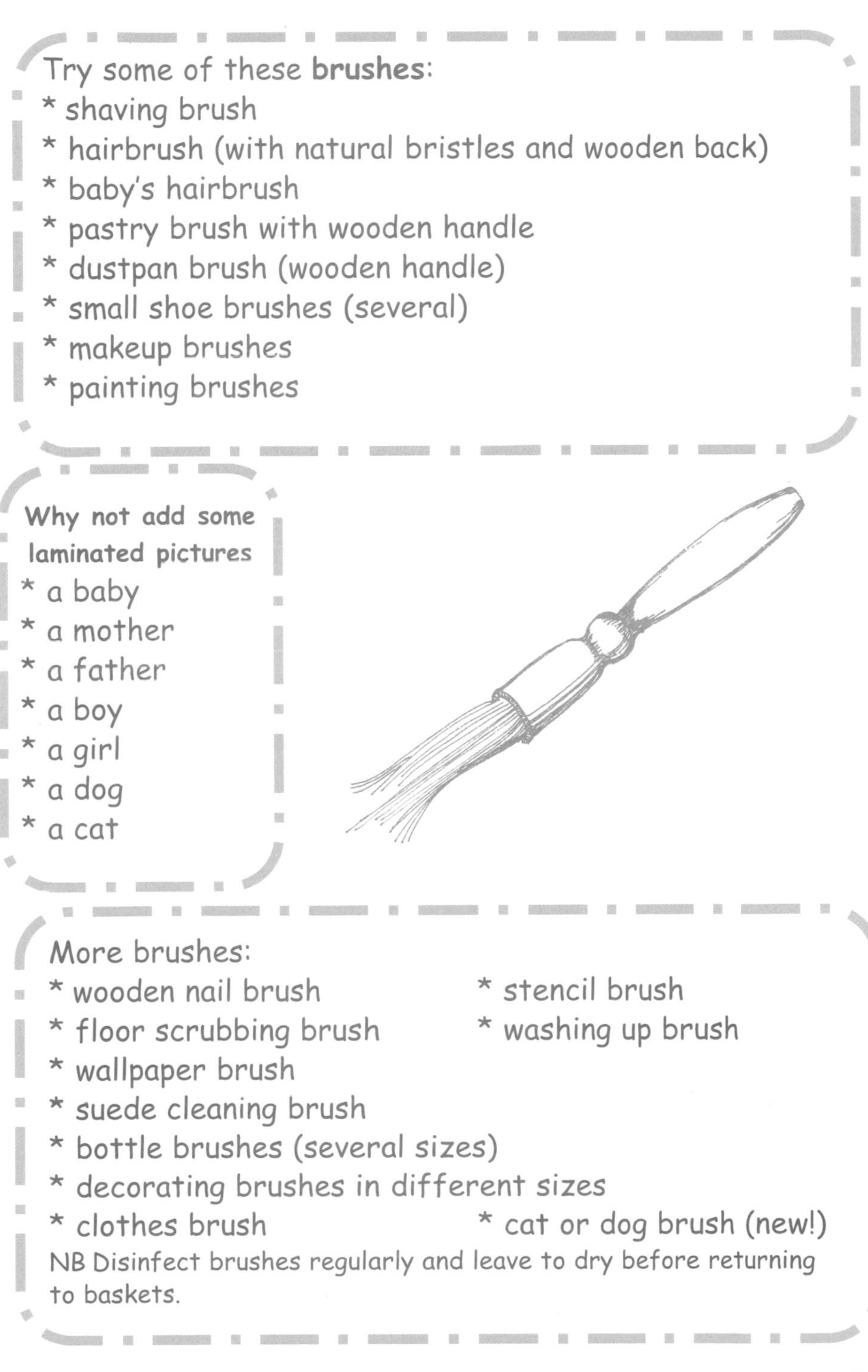

More brushes:

* wooden nail brush
* floor scrubbing brush
* wallpaper brush
* suede cleaning brush
* bottle brushes (several sizes)
* decorating brushes in different sizes
* clothes brush
* stencil brush
* washing up brush
* cat or dog brush (new!)

NB Disinfect brushes regularly and leave to dry before returning to baskets.

The collections in Part 2 can be extended to all areas of the curriculum, linked to your planning and to the developing interests of the children.

Treasure baskets for older children can help them to explore the following areas:

Baskets can contain creative stimuli, musical objects, festival treasures, collections for shape, number and colour, themed items or objects to develop fine motor skills. The use of phonic, story and language baskets is steadily growing in Foundation Stage settings, and this can greatly extend independent communication, language and literacy experiences for 3, 4 and 5 year olds.

For example, in personal and social development, a Treasure Basket could help children to:

- continue to be interested, excited & motivated to learn
- maintain attention, concentration & sit quietly when appropriate;
- have a developing respect for their own cultures & beliefs & those of other people;
- select & use activities & resources independently.

In communication, language & literacy, a Treasure Basket could help to:

- extend their vocabulary, exploring the meaning & sounds of new words;
- use language to imagine & recreate roles & experiences;
- hear & say initial sounds in words, short vowel sounds within words;
- link letters & sounds, naming & sounding letters of the alphabet;
- explore and experiment with sounds, words and texts;
- retell narratives in the correct sequence.

In mathematical concepts, a Treasure Basket could help children to:

- say and use number names in order in familiar contexts;
- count reliably up to 10 everyday objects;
- use language such as greater, smaller, heavier or lighter to compare objects;
- use everyday words to describe position;
- talk about, recognise and recreate simple patterns.

- use language such as circle, or bigger to describe the shape and size of solids and flat shapes;

In knowledge and understanding of the world, a Treasure Basket could help children to:

- investigate objects & materials by using all of their senses;
- find out about, & identify some features of living things, objects and events they observe;
- look closely at similarities, differences, patterns;
- find out about past & present events in their own lives and in those of their families & other people they know;
- observe, find out & identify features in the natural world;
- begin to know about their own cultures & beliefs & those of others.

In physical development, a Treasure Basket could help children to:

- move with control and co-ordination;
- use a range of small and large equipment;
- handle tools, objects, construction & malleable materials safely and with increasing control.

In creative development, a Treasure Basket could help children to:

- explore colour, texture, shape, form & space in two and three dimensions;
- recognise and explore how sounds can be changed
- respond in a variety of ways to what they see, hear, smell, touch and feel.

Of course, practitioners need to know that all activities help children to make progress towards the Early Learning Goals. However, we must not forget **the major purposes** of the baskets described in this book -

* to give children free and unfettered access to collections of tactile materials and objects of interest
* to give children free choice in the way they select and combine the objects we offer
* to allow children to reflect on, explore and discuss materials and objects with each other, with as little interference as possible from adults, once the collection has been presented.

N.B. Elinor Goldschmied's baskets for babies only include natural materials. Some of the suggestions for baskets for older children do include some plastic and other man made objects. If you wish to follow the philosophy strictly, you should not include these objects.

A Sense of Smell

Smell is a powerful sense, and one which we offer less frequently than the others. Older babies and children love to have things to smell, and may become very attached to certain perfumes and perfumed objects.

The addition of smelling jars and bags enables you to offer sensations without the need to intervene in their use.

Older children will enjoy guessing what is in the jars and bags.

Because there is a risk that the contents of this basket might be tasted, it may be wiser to offer it to older children who are able to understand about what they can eat!

N.B. Check for any allergies before deciding what to include in this basket.

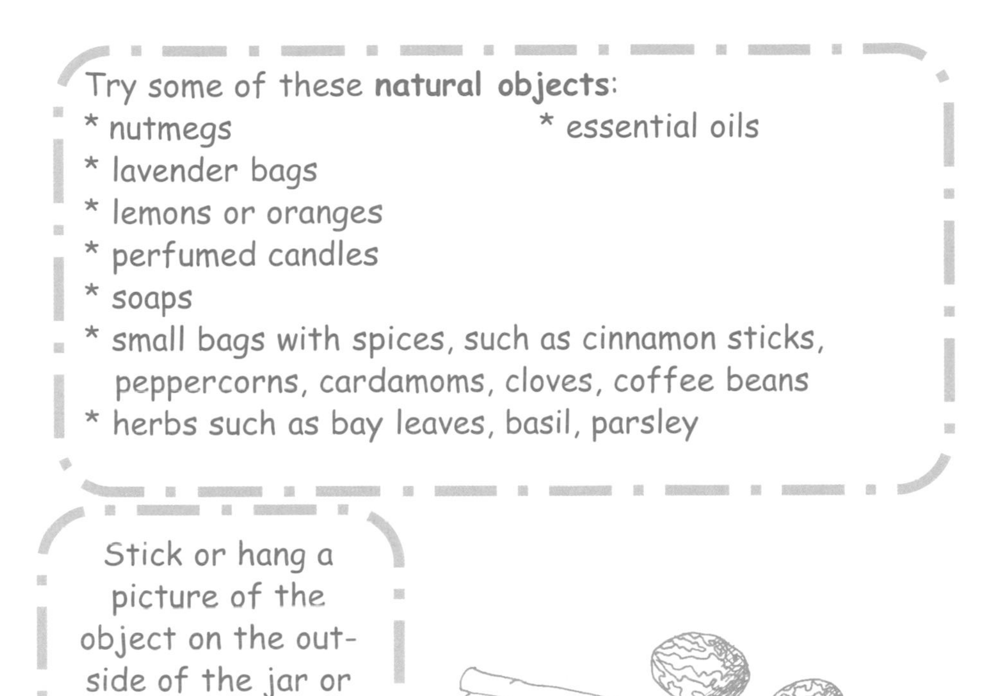

Try some of these **natural objects**:

* nutmegs
* lavender bags
* lemons or oranges
* perfumed candles
* soaps
* small bags with spices, such as cinnamon sticks, peppercorns, cardamoms, cloves, coffee beans
* herbs such as bay leaves, basil, parsley
* essential oils

Stick or hang a picture of the object on the outside of the jar or bag.

Add to your collection with herb filled pillows and soft toys

Smelling Jars

Make some smelling jars from small jars. Baby food jars are ideal.

Put a few drops of massage oil, peppermint oil, rose water or perfume on a piece of cotton wool in each jar.

Make a few holes in the lids with a hammer and nail and fix securely on each jar.

Gauze fastened with an elastic band also works.

A Sound of Music

This basket is for budding musicians and could be used indoors or out. You don't need bought instruments to make music, so start with natural materials. You can then add a few simple instruments, making them with the children or buying a few at a time to build up a collection.

Give the children plenty of time to explore the sound makers by themselves, before adding instruments.

A useful addition is a simple tape recorder with nursery rhymes and songs, or a short piece of atmospheric music. Teach the children how to use this by themselves and they can add the tape to their own music or play an accompaniment to the tape.

Try some of these **natural sound makers**:

* paper
* dry leaves
* sandpaper
* foil
* ribbons to wave
* thick bamboo
* small boxes, tubes, tins filled with stones, rice etc
* curtain rings (wood or metal) on a string
* chain
* wooden baby rattles
* wooden beads on a string
* a small rain stick
* small blocks of wood
* empty tins & boxes

Music making is noisy! You may want to offer this basket for use outside on a blanket, or at a time when the resulting sounds can be managed.

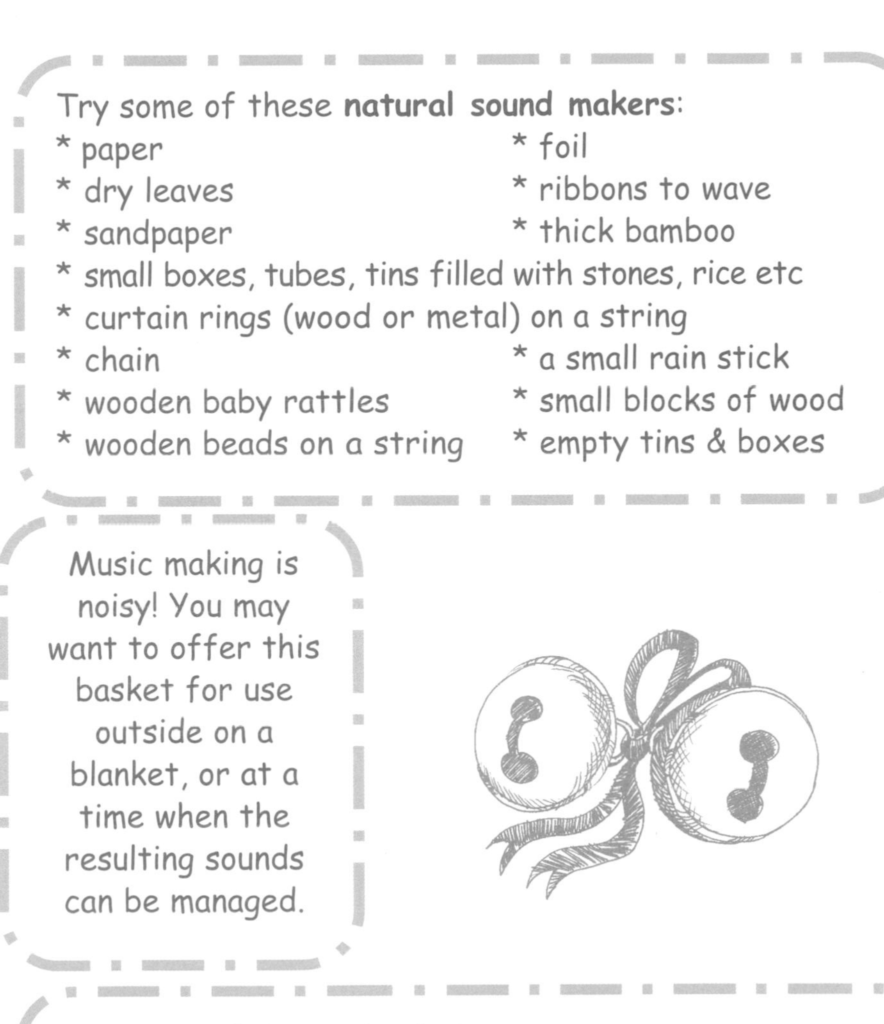

Try some of these simple instruments:

* bells
* triangles
* wind chimes
* chime bars
* claves or rhythm sticks
* chopsticks, pencils
* shakers and maracas
* castanets
* small drum
* guiro
* tambourine
* bird whistle
* kazoos
* small bongo drums
* sandpaper blocks
* click-clacks

A Sense of Time

Children can develop a sense of time by handling objects which belonged to their parents when they were children. These are not museum objects, just objects that are not in regular use now.

This basket gives children a chance to explore and handle objects from another age. Many can be bought from charity shops or rummage sales for a small amount, or you may know of a shop which still sells these things. You could also try asking parents and carers if they or their families have things to donate to the History basket.

Schools also often have old weights, coins and other memorabilia which can add to your collection.

Start with some of these **household objects and clothes**:

* old cameras
* a lavatory chain and handle
* fabric handkerchiefs
* an apron
* a fountain pen
* old postcards
* a locket
* a school satchel
* bicycle clips
* old coins
* braces or a snake belt
* baby toys and rattles
* old photos
* an old telephone

Old photos and pictures give added interest to this basket.
You may also want to spend time introducing and discussing the contents.

Old fashioned toys:

* wooden animals
* tin and other metal cars
* an old teddy bear
* an old doll
* clockwork toys
* a slate and chalk
* marbles
* a skipping rope
* fivestones
* a china teaset
* an old doll
* cloth or board books
* a top
* a wooden or rag doll
* knitted baby clothes
* old board games

Light and Colour

Exploring by looking into and through transparent and coloured materials is a fascinating experience for children.

Looking into a paperweight or making the world turn red through cellophane paper, seeing a reflection in a spoon, or wearing coloured glasses all expand children's knowledge and understanding of the world around them.

Adding torches, mirrors, kaleidoscopes all extend the fun, and if you put the basket in a strong light, the children will be able to explore shadows and reflections as well.

Make sure that all glass objects are tough enough to withstand handling.

Try some of these **objects**:

* a hand mirror
* shiny metal objects
* foil
* shiny spoons
* small coloured glass jars and bottles
* coloured glass beads
* paperweights
* a piece of curtain net
* sunglasses
* clear containers
* CD cases
* small sand timer
* old glasses frames with cellophane lenses
* coloured cellophane

Hang some objects from strings in front of a window or a light, and let the children explore the resulting shadows.
Try a prism or a glass wind chime.

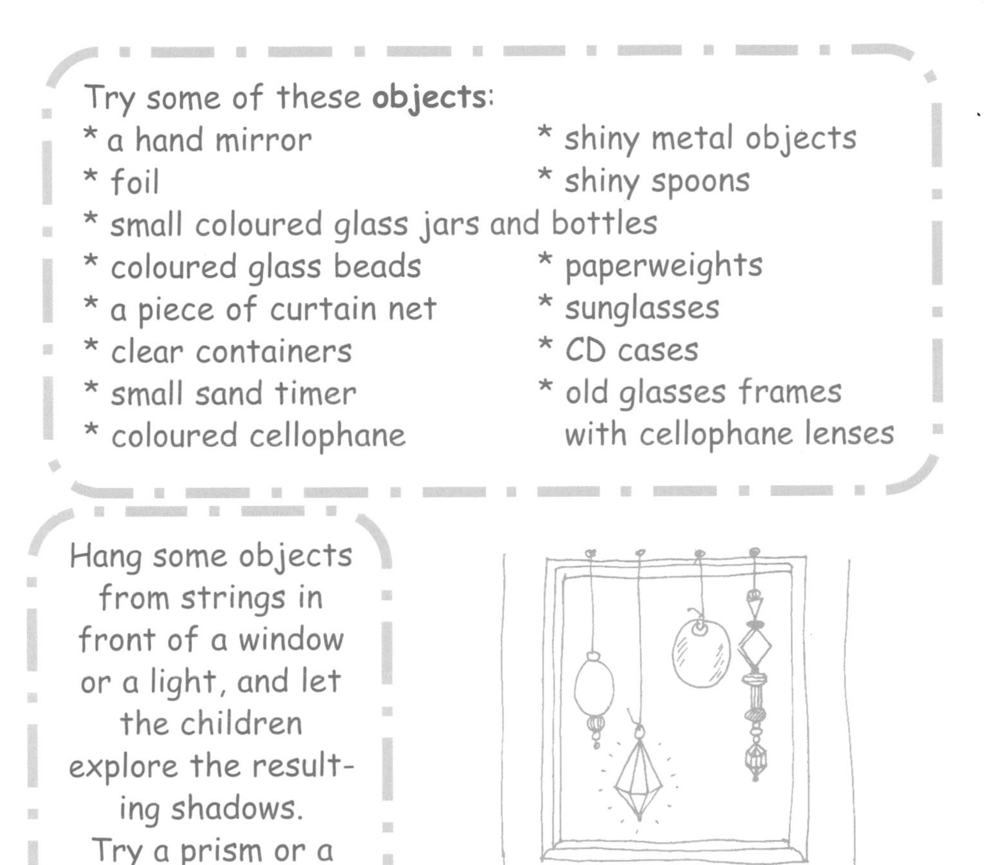

Then add some of these:

* a prism
* a torch
* pieces of coloured perspex
* balloons
* tissue/greaseproof paper
* shadow puppets
* old glasses frames
* net or gauze
* a telescope
* a kaleidoscope
* plastic mirrors
* bubble wrap
* a jar of bubbles
* black paper
* plastic bottles filled with coloured liquids

Light and Heavy

The exploration of weight and mass is an important part of science for young children. This collection should contain extremes of weight as well as pairs of similar objects with different weights.

Physical exploration of the contents of such a basket should come before the abstract concepts of comparison and balance.

Children of all ages love picking up and handling heavy things and can do this safely if seated on a rug or carpet (or on the grass outside). The lighter things provided can be shaken, waved or tossed in the air.

This basket could be combined with the 'Will it float?' basket.

Try some of these **objects**:

* big stones
* a weight for scales
* wood pieces
* a paperweight
* a glass bottle
* a can of beans
* a hardback book
* a metal toy car
* feathers
* leaves
* paper
* an empty film can
* a plastic bottle
* an empty bean can
* a paperback
* a plastic toy car
* bubbles
* picnic cup
* gauze
* tissue paper

Suitable fabrics

* net, gauze
* gauze
* silk
* sari material
* chiffon scarves
* flags and bunting
* crepe paper streamers

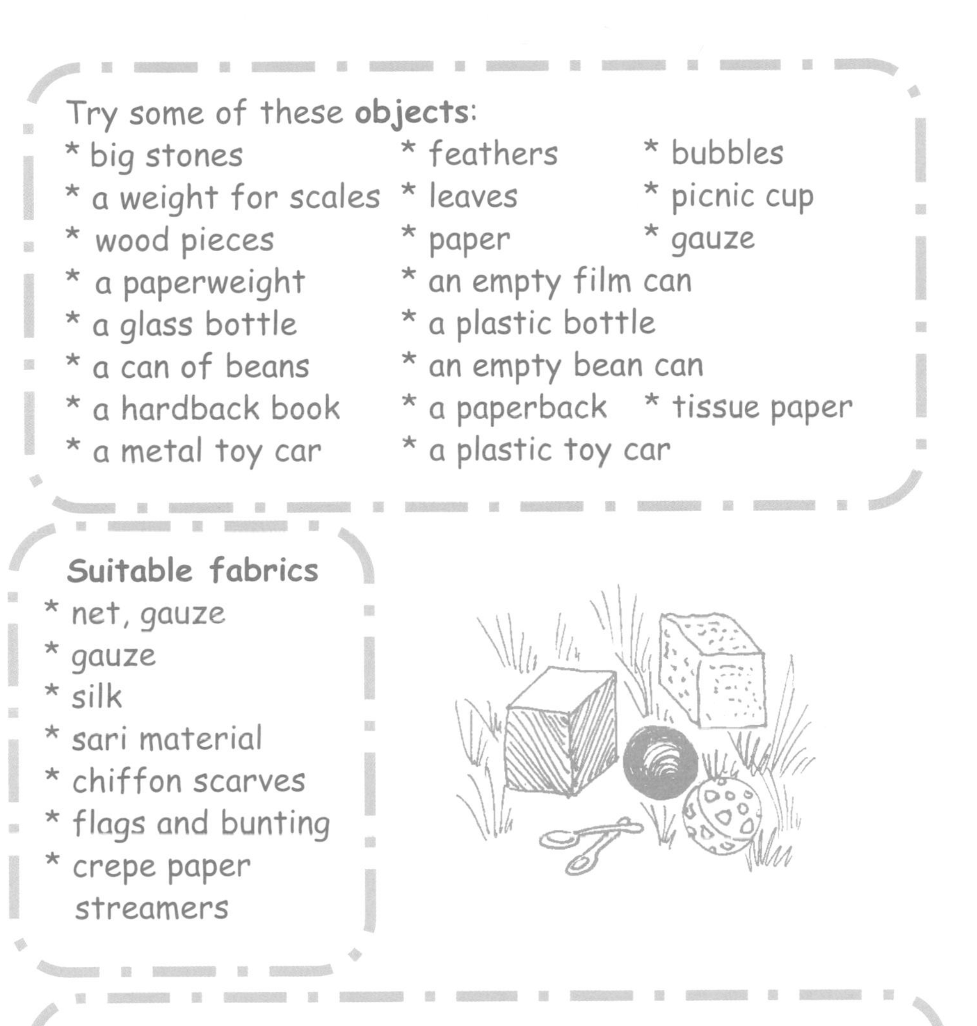

This basket is particularly suited for use out of doors, where the light, floaty objects can be watched and enjoyed. There is also a place for a variety of gauzy, floaty fabrics, ribbons and streamers, which the children can explore by running, tossing, waving, floating and twirling.

The concept of heavy things can also be explored outside, if children are involved in getting out and putting away equipment and toys. However, take care!

The Magnetic Basket

This basket offers free access to scientific exploration. You might want to tie the magnet on to the basket with a long string to make sure it can be easily retrieved from the basket.

It would be best <u>not</u> to introduce this activity - just leave the basket for them to discover and watch what happens. Some of the objects are small and some are sharp - use your discretion when you assemble the basket, take into account the age and stage of the children and leave out things you are doubtful about- remember "when in doubt, leave it out."

You might also like to put this basket on a small table outside.

Start with some of these:

* a horseshoe magnet
* washers
* tin lids
* paper clips
* small pieces of wood
* a plastic cup
* pencil
* a small plastic bottle
* nails and screws
* nuts and bolts
* drawing pins
* cotton reels
* fir cones
* paper
* wooden shapes
* a stone

Make sure that some of the metal things in the basket can not be picked up by the magnet! Aluminium items and most coins would be suitable.

Now add these:

* some more magnets
* a baking tray and some magnetic letters
* metal badges
* costume jewellery
* a copper bracelet
* a piece of wood
* scissors
* a butter knife
* fridge magnets
* a bicycle bell
* stainless steel spoon
* a duster
* a nail file
* a shiny plastic bauble

Feel This

This 'feely' basket, contains all sorts of textures and fabrics to feel. Many children will need to feel the fabrics on their faces, arms and legs a well as their hands.

Older children can be encouraged to develop the language of texture through this basket. They associate texture much more with their feelings and experiences than many adults do, so be aware of this as you watch and listen to their responses. Make a swatch of small pieces of fabrics, so the children can look at it like a book.

These fabrics may need more frequent washing/ cleaning as they will be used as comfort and security objects by some children.

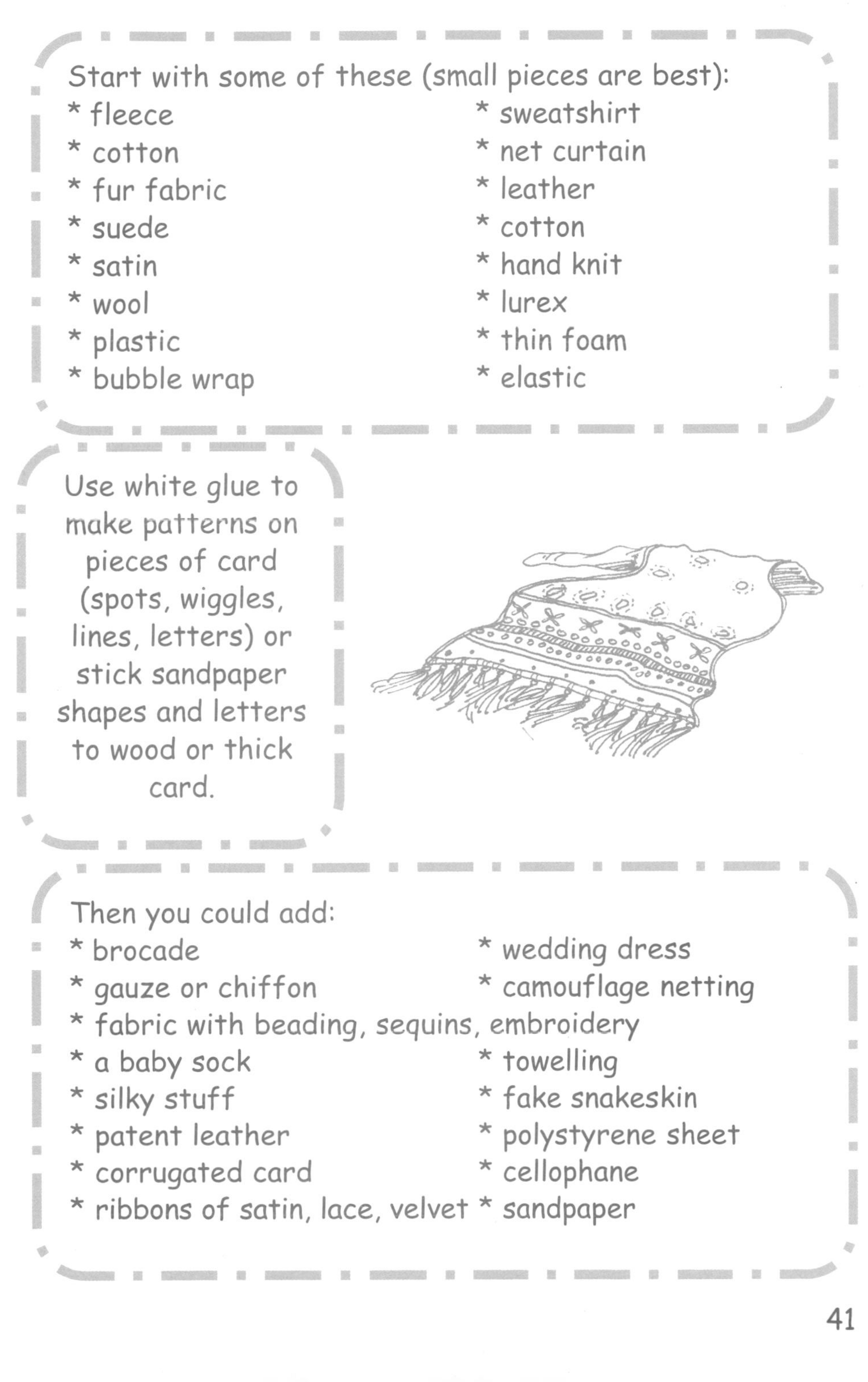

Start with some of these (small pieces are best):

* fleece
* cotton
* fur fabric
* suede
* satin
* wool
* plastic
* bubble wrap
* sweatshirt
* net curtain
* leather
* cotton
* hand knit
* lurex
* thin foam
* elastic

Use white glue to make patterns on pieces of card (spots, wiggles, lines, letters) or stick sandpaper shapes and letters to wood or thick card.

Then you could add:

* brocade
* wedding dress
* gauze or chiffon
* camouflage netting
* fabric with beading, sequins, embroidery
* a baby sock
* towelling
* silky stuff
* fake snakeskin
* patent leather
* polystyrene sheet
* corrugated card
* cellophane
* ribbons of satin, lace, velvet
* sandpaper

Will it Float?

Floating and sinking, waterlogging and deluging. If you discuss this with the children, they can use the objects to help with prediction and experimentation.

Similar objects (2 balls, 2 cups) one that sinks, one that floats will encourage discrimination and discussion as pairs or groups work independently with this basket.

You may want to put a waterproof liner in the basket (or use one designed for plants) in order to reduce the water leakage.

You could also put the basket outside with a bowl of water for experiments.

Of course, you will need to replace those items which disintegrate when immersed!

Start with these:

* paper
* a plastic bottle
* a shell
* bubble wrap
* a ping pong ball
* a metal car
* a cup
* a pencil
* polystyrene 'wiggles'
* a stone
* a feather
* a big nail
* a golf ball
* a plastic car
* a funnel
* a coin

This basket could be located near the water tray, indoors or out, with encouragement to experiment.

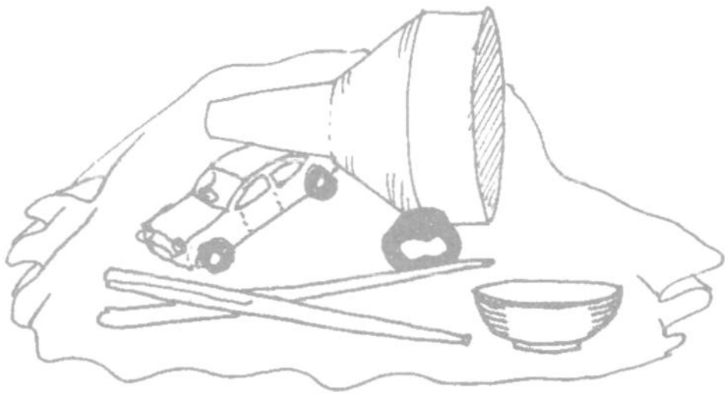

Then add some of these:

* a piece of wood
* a cardboard tube
* a chopstick
* a sock
* a wooden brick
* a piece of foam
* a plastic Christmas bauble
* a conker
* a fir cone
* a paper bag
* an apple
* a plastic brick
* china saucer
* paper clip
* an elastic band
* a walnut

Put It In

This basket starts with containers without lids, making for easy access and opening for the younger children. When they have mastered the containers, or for older children, add lids for the containers and some more with hinged lids. The small things could either be offered in cloth bags or loose in the basket.

A lined basket enables you to include smaller objects and multiples of things like pasta shapes, beads, coins, stones and shells without losing them.

Some children get very involved in this activity and will spend considerable lengths of time absorbed in it - repeatedly filling and emptying the containers.
This is a normal stage of development (a schema) - don't stop them!

Start with some of these:

* a cup
* a plastic bottle
* a matchbox
* a sweet tube (no top)
* a toilet roll tube
* a spectacle case
* a tin (no lid)
* a bowl
* a small saucepan
* box (no lid)
* a piece of hose
* a purse
* small items such as small world people, coins, beads, wooden small cars, large dry pasta shapes, nuts, etc

Some contents of the basket may be specific to one container (e.g. a ring and a ring box) but don't make it an intelligence test! Let them choose what goes where.

Then add some of these:

* a jar with a screw top
* a lid for the saucepan
* a box with a lid
* plastic bottles with tops
* a pen case
* a tin with a lid
* a plastic teapot
* small cloth bags
* a watch box
* a ring box
* a wooden box with a hinged lid
* nesting dolls
* an egg box (with wooden eggs)
* suitable objects to fit in the containers you add

Sort the Sound

The Treasure Basket approach is particularly suited to introducing phonic collections - using single sounds at first.

Encourage the children to contribute to the phonic baskets and give a clue by hanging a clear, unambiguous picture label on the edge of the basket. A snake is unambiguous - a sweet could be confusing for some children!

Use your discretion and knowledge of the children in your group to decide whether you could use two baskets at once or several over a week - double baskets may not be appropriate before the Reception year or for children who are learning English as an additional language.

A 'b' basket might contain:

* a ball
* some buttons
* a badge
* a fabric or metal butterfly
* a bowl
* a toy bike
* binoculars
* a brick
* a box
* a belt
* a baby's bib
* a bandage
* a bucket
* a string of beads
* a biscuit
* a brooch & bracelet

Combine the contents of two baskets for a phonic sorting activity. You could offer the children two smaller baskets to sort the things into as they name them.

An 's' basket might contain:

* a sandal
* a can of soup
* a snake
* a saucepan
* a snail shell
* a stamp
* a skittle
* scissors
* a slipper
* a seed
* a strawberry
* a stone
* a spoon
* a spider
* sequins
* a sweet

Sparkle and Shine

This basket could support celebrations (such as Diwali or Christmas) or just to brighten up a winter day.

Children love sparkle (you could spray the basket silver or gold, or line it with shiny material) and some will spend considerable time exploring and talking about the contents.

Small transparent boxes or bags of sequins, glitter, shiny beads or buttons will also interest some children. The constant surprise of using these baskets is that you can't predict which children will choose to play with them, or which objects they will select to play with. Observing them will give many clues to their feelings, needs and stage of development.

Start with some of these:

* a mirror
* shiny paper
* sweet papers
* spoons
* tinsel
* lametta
* shiny fabrics
* shiny beads
* unbreakable Christmas decorations
* sequins of various sizes and shapes in small bags and boxes
* foil (different colours)

Shiny fabric makes a good base for exploring the items in the basket as children take them out, and magnifying glasses, mirrors and kaleidoscope viewers all make the sparkle more vivid.

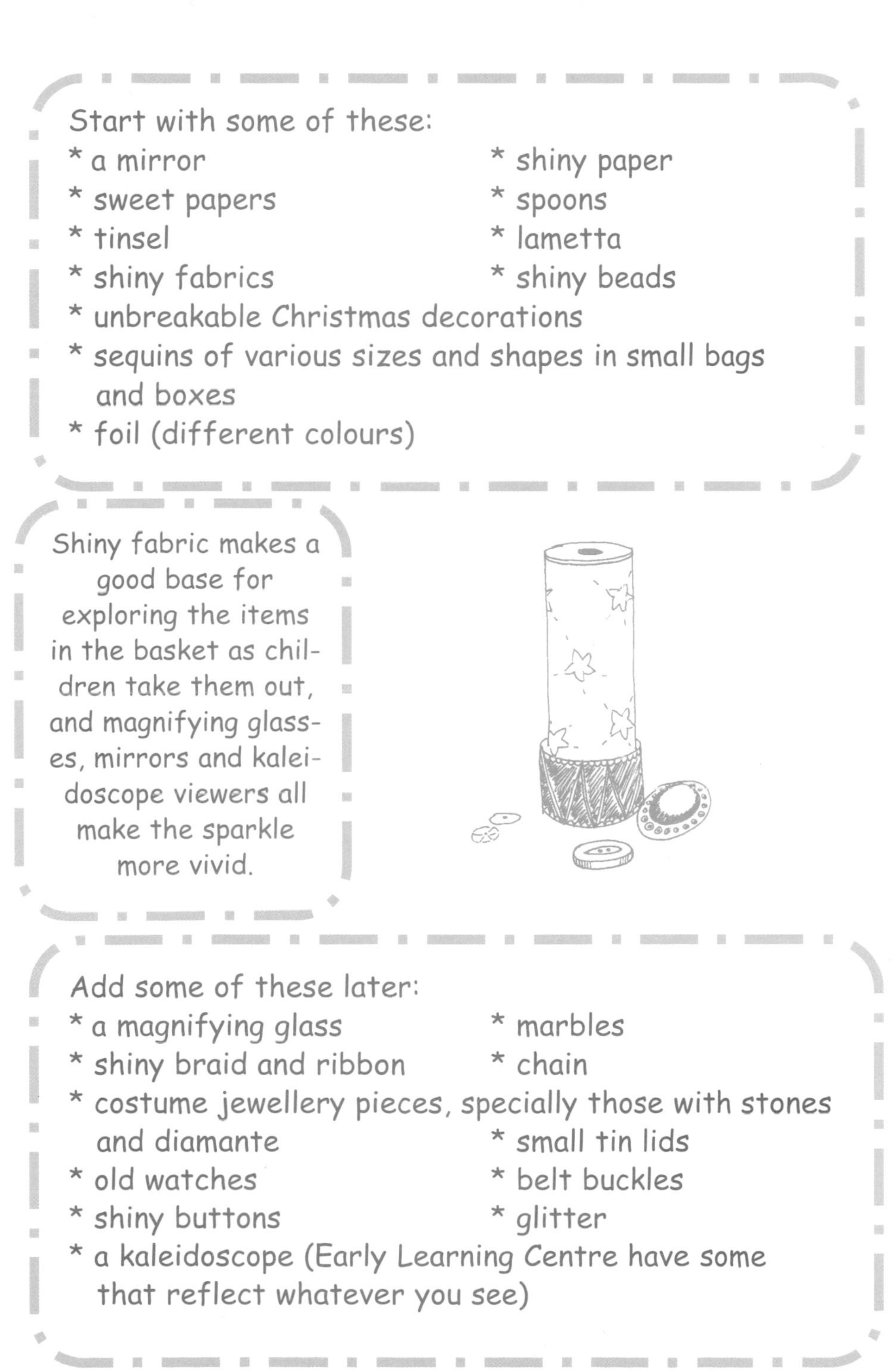

Add some of these later:

* a magnifying glass
* marbles
* shiny braid and ribbon
* chain
* costume jewellery pieces, specially those with stones and diamante
* small tin lids
* old watches
* belt buckles
* shiny buttons
* glitter
* a kaleidoscope (Early Learning Centre have some that reflect whatever you see)

A Basket Full of Colour

Colour baskets are good fun to collect and, if they contain varied objects, they can stimulate all the senses.

Involve the children in collecting the objects, flavours, shades and scents, collect and add pictures and drawings (perhaps in a 'slip sleeve' photo album).

Go for a colour walk or a colour hunt in the garden or your community - take a camera and add some photos to your collection.

Use small jars for shades of paint, capture cooked or uncooked pasta in zip lock bags and colour it with food colouring. Make coloured dough to include in bags.

Here are some starter objects for your colour baskets.

Fruit & vegetables

* apple * orange
* mango * banana
* carrot * onion
* potato * peas
* sweet potato
* okra * plums
* cauliflower * grapes

Herbs and spices

* parsley * mint
* garlic * cloves
* root ginger
* cinnamon sticks
* coriander seeds
* star anise

Fabrics and clothes

* silver shoes
* blue jeans * red fleece
* brown belt * black tie
* purple velvet
* yellow raincoat
* gold lame
* green wellies

Toys

* red fire engine
* black horse
* purple marble
* green Lego tree
* brown dinosaur
* blue brick
* orange ball

Household objects

* silver scissors
* brass doorknob
* yellow duster
* brown clothes peg
* red bowl
* blue glass vase
* green scourer

Other places to look

* Christmas decorations
* felt pens and crayons
* buttons and buckles
* beads and bricks
* feathers, ribbon
* small world, cars,
  construction toys

All Sorts of Shapes

These baskets give children opportunities to compare and sort. They can either contain one type of shape (for instance the things with holes) or a mixture of two types. Beyond two types, the basket just becomes a collection of random objects!

As before, children will enjoy adding to the collection by bringing objects from home or from around the room and in the garden.

When you introduce a new basket or contents, be careful that you don't imply that there is only one 'right' way to use it. Keep your introduction brief, saying you have put some new things in the basket, and showing them where it will be if they want to use it. Let them explore and discover.

Circles and spheres
* ball
* orange
* beads
* marbles
* plates
* saucers
* CDs
* baubles
* washers
* buttons
* wool pom poms
* tin/jar tops

Things with holes
* washers
* rings
* beads
* pasta
* sequin waste
* net
* buttons
* stones and shells
* cotton reels
* nuts and bolts

Long and short
* a long and short ruler
* lengths of ribbon
* string
* wool
* pencils
* straws
* nails and screws
* keys
* sticks
* paper strips

Big and small
* shoes
* socks
* gloves
* boxes
* toy cars
* tins
* keys
* washers
* teddies
* balls
* plastic bottles
* lids
* spoons

Rectangles and cuboids
* envelopes
* boxes
* matchboxes
* bricks
* CD cases

Squares & cubes
* bricks
* boxes
* stock cubes
* dice

Cylinders
* empty cans
* straws
* tubes
* big candles
* tubing
* corks
* empty tablet tubs
* tops from aerosols
* hair rollers

A Sense of Place

Replace some of your displays with baskets of objects meant to be handled and rearranged!

These baskets give children opportunities to think of places - real or imagined. Some are associated with holidays, others with stories, some with occasions, others with people, and of course many will link with current projects or topics, visits and outings.

The secret is to remember that children learn more if they use all their senses, not just sight. Try to include a stimulus for each sense in each collection.

Once you start these baskets, the children will suggest more, and you will be able to use your imagination and ingenuity to make a regular feature of such baskets in your setting.

All at sea

* shells
* beach ball
* swimsuit
* small towel
* bucket
* postcards
* pebbles
* flip flops
* arm bands
* a small world seaside scene

It's the Bear

* hamper for a basket
* 2 plates, 2 cups
* tablecloth
* food made from salt dough
* 2 teddies (big & small)

The zoo visit

* a toy coach
* zoo animals
* cages or fences
* play people
* camera
* play mat
* tickets

Autumn walk

* leaves
* twigs
* acorns
* conkers
* dried corn on the cob
* chinese lanterns
* tree and shrub seeds (check safety)
* bark

Lets Celebrate Christmas

* holly and fir sprigs
* spices in bags
* cards
* bells
* candles
* baubles
* wooden ornaments
* gift boxes
* nuts

Kay's New Baby Came

* baby bottle
* clothes
* cards
* baby food jars
* rattle or baby toys
* nappies
* photos
* baby toiletries
* baby catalogues

Maintaining Basket Collections

As with any resource, safety should be paramount, and risk assessment regularly undertaken. However, this does not mean restricting children's access to a wide range of everyday materials and objects to explore. We must be vigilant (that is why adults must be on hand, particularly when young babies are using Treasure Baskets), but not too cautious. Here are a few suggestions.

1. Swallowing risks. If you are worried about any of the things you choose to include in a basket, put the object in your own mouth. If you can't swallow it, then neither can the baby. "If in doubt, leave it out" is a good motto!
2. Long handles. Small babies are very careful with the objects they handle. The risk increases as they get a bit older and start to test things by banging, scraping and poking with them. Watch the children, and if you are worried, remove long handled objects or cut the handles down.
3. Of course, you check all equipment for sharp edges and corners, splinters and other wear and tear. Treasure Baskets need this regular check as well, and items which cause concern must be discarded.
4. Perishable or expendable items such as fruit or paper items need to be replaced as soon as they look worn - otherwise the basket will soon lose its appeal.
5. What about the germs? Anything that can be washed, should be washed regularly. Items that cannot be immersed in water need wiping with a damp cloth and disinfectant.

Storage

If you collect objects over time, you can have one or more baskets in use at any time, you can combine collections and make up new ones.

The objects can be stored in the baskets, but this can cause problems if they don't stack securely, and of course, the baskets themselves can be an expense. Practitioners in settings where Treasure Baskets are regularly in use find it more convenient to store items not currently in use in one of the following ways:

* labelled shoe boxes, or other boxes with lids, one for each collection
* drawstring bags which can be hung on the back of a door or in a cupboard
* plastic stacking crates or boxes (a cheaper option, but more likely to attract dust!)
* plastic 'book bag' type containers (the advantage being that you can see the contents).

Costs

Of course, there is no such thing as a free item of equipment, but Treasure Baskets can be a very cost effective resource, particularly if you collect them over time.

Some objects are free - collected on walks and excursions, recycled from 'junk', or or donated by parents, staff and friends;

Some are cheap, acquired from charity shops or in sales;

Some are pieces of household equipment, made to last and lasting in use;

and some (relatively few) have to be bought specially, or regularly replaced.

The majority of the contents in the Treasure Baskets in this book will cost you small amounts to buy. If you have limited funds, concentrate on one or two well stocked baskets - your children will have just as much fun with these. Early years people are inventive, always on the lookout for a bargain, a substitute or an alternative. Just hold on to the principles of the baskets - to:

* to encourage children to use of all their senses
* to introduce the children to a wide range of natural materials
* to balance the use of bright colours and man made materials with the subtle colours, textures and shapes of natural objects
* to use collections of familiar objects to stimulate play
* to provide opportunities for children to make choices and develop preferences from a very young age
* to stimulate movement, communication and language through simple materials.

Bibliography

Title	Author	Publisher	ISBN
* Infants at Work	Elinor Goldschmied	NCB (1987)	
* People Under Three	Elinor Goldschmied & Sonia Jackson	Routledge	0-415-05976-3

Videos

* Infants at Work	Elinor Goldschmied	NCB (1989)	
* Heuristic Play with Objects	Elinor Goldschmied & Anita Hughes	NCB (1992)	
* I Don't Need Toys	Anita Hughes, 1 Oakland Close, Shalford, Surrey, GU4 8JL		

Did you enjoy this Little Book?
Would you like to see some more?

Then join

The Little Books Club!

There's a new Little Book each month. The best way to see the new titles is to join The Little Books Club.

- ***Members get each new book on approval before it goes on general sale***
- ***Costs nothing to join***
- ***NO MINIMUM PURCHASE***
- ***Only pay for the books you choose to keep***
- ***Discounts on bookshop prices, plus special offers***

Interested?

Phone Featherstone Education

0185 888 1212

for a free information pack and enrolment form